My Favourite Beach

By Michael Torres

Library For All Ltd.

Library For All is an Australian not for profit organisation with a mission to make knowledge accessible to all via an innovative digital library solution. Visit us at libraryforall.org

My Favourite Beach

First published 2023

Published by Library For All Ltd
Email: info@libraryforall.org
URL: libraryforall.org

Our Yarning logo design by Jason Lee, Bidjipidji Art

Original illustrations by keishart

My Favourite Beach
Torres, Michael
ISBN: 978-1-923110-17-5
SKU03370

My Favourite Beach

We respect and honour Aboriginal and Torres Strait Islander Elders past, present and future. We acknowledge the stories, traditions and living cultures of Aboriginal and Torres Strait Islander peoples on this land and commit to building a brighter future together.

Sam and I walked over the sand dunes to the beach. There were seagulls sitting on their nests, keeping their eggs safe.

We skipped along the sand, laughing at our shadows.

While we walked
along the beach,
ghost crabs ran
between our toes.

Sam screamed and jumped away as the crabs sprinted across the sand.

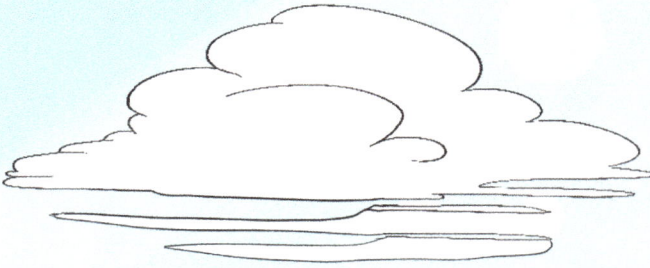

We skipped to our favourite part of the beach and gathered driftwood to build a cubbyhouse.

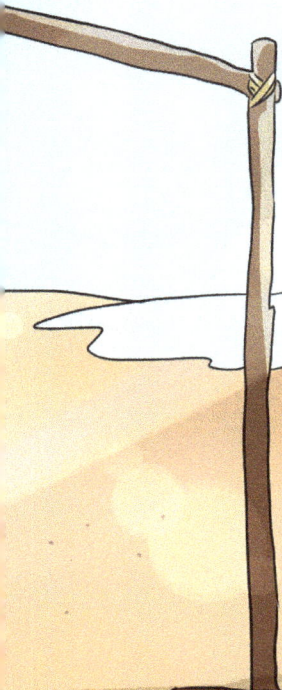

I pushed the sticks into the sand and Sam tied them together. We built a cubbyhouse in ten minutes.

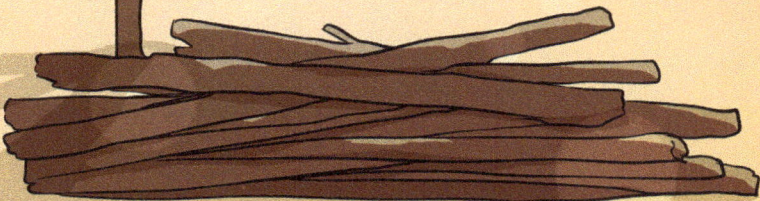

Sam dug a ditch around
the cubbyhouse, and I
filled it with water.

We named it 'The King's Castle' and made a wall out of sticks to defend ourselves from pirates.

I walked to the water's edge to fill my bucket. As I filled the bucket, several small fish swam inside it.

I raced back to the castle and poured the water and fish into the ditch. The fish swam around like it was their home.

We dug a hole between the sandcastles and filled it with water. Sam made boats out of driftwood, and we sailed them in our little lake.

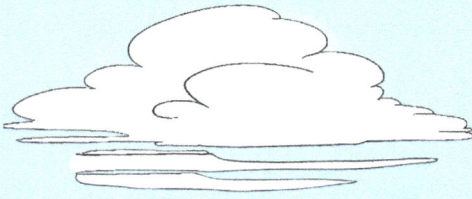

Sam shovelled sand into the buckets, while I squashed the sand down with my feet. We tipped the buckets up to make sandcastles.

We walked along the beach collecting shells. I found a dead starfish. Sam found a crab shell.

We pushed the shells into the sandy walls and placed the starfish on the top of the sandcastle.

When we finished our sandcastle building, I raced Sam along the beach and we swam in the cool sea, splashing and jumping over the waves. I dived like a dolphin and Sam swam like a shark.

We played around the sandy
castle and eventually fell asleep.
I dreamed of big fat turtles
clambering up the beach.

Suddenly my mother woke me and grabbed me by the hand. It was time to go home and leave my favourite beach.

You can use these questions to talk about this book with your family, friends and teachers.

What did you learn from this book?

Describe this book in one word. Funny? Scary? Colourful? Interesting?

How did this book make you feel when you finished reading it?

What was your favourite part of this book?

download our reader app
getlibraryforall.org

About the author

Michael was born and lives in Darwin; he is from the Jabirr Jabirr Nation north of Broome, Western Australia. He loves family gatherings, and playing games with his grandchildren at the beach and playgrounds.

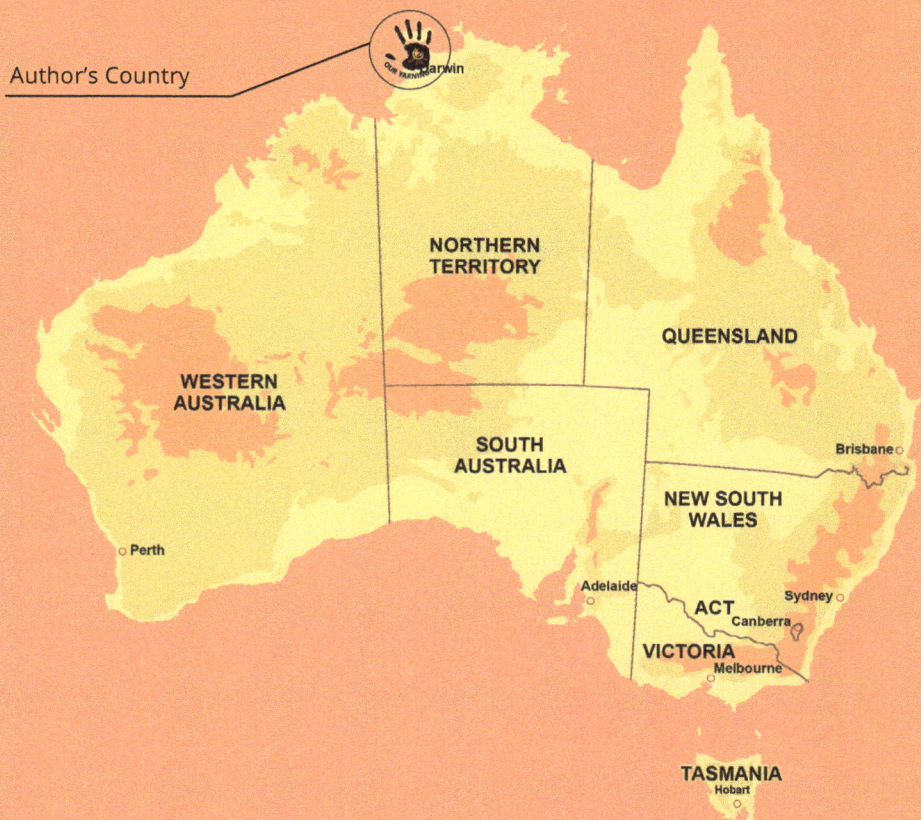

Author's Country

Darwin

NORTHERN TERRITORY

QUEENSLAND

WESTERN AUSTRALIA

SOUTH AUSTRALIA

Brisbane

NEW SOUTH WALES

Perth

Adelaide

Sydney

ACT
Canberra

VICTORIA
Melbourne

TASMANIA
Hobart

Our Yarning

Want to discover more books from this collection? Our Yarning is a collection of books written by Aboriginal and Torres Strait Islander peoples across Australia.

We know that children learn better, and enjoy reading more, when they see themselves in the stories, characters and illustrations of the books they read.

To download the app, visit the Google Play Store on any Android device and search 'Our Yarning'.

libraryforall.org